French Country Style
at Home

For Joseph and Lucien, and for Laure, my most attentive reader
and inspirational companion in our own country life.

French Country Style at Home

Texts and photographs by Sébastien Siraudeau

Flammarion

Contents

Country living. A new take on an old dream. Two words to be greeted like a delightful, long-expected invitation. Today we eat organic, think sustainability, and have a duty to act on our ideas. We flirt with eco-lifestyles. We have heeded the wake-up call, to act now in our daily lives for the good of generations to come—so far in the future, and so near. In cities, towns, and countryside, people are opening their eyes to the environment, doing their bit for the good of the earth. We sort our trash, we recycle and recoup. It's essential. We swap, scout for secondhand items, restore vintage objects and antiques. For fun, as gifts, to make a statement. Bric-a-brac style. Every object has a moving or happy story to share. Places, too. Each home tells the story of a life. Or several lives. An eclectic mix of genres and styles hints at bohemian tastes, the desire to break free that lies dormant at the back of every mind. An instinct for freedom and independence, flourishing closer to home. Short breaks away, even a simple change of scenery at home: more inner space, new colors to transform your interior. Escape still means travel, too, of course. But you don't have to circumnavigate the globe. Elsewhere begins on your doorstep. The skyline of a grassy field, a country road, a forest, a modest mountain. We're rediscovering the simple life, getting back to basics, to nature, to authentic local lifestyles, exploring unexpected territories. Some have taken the plunge and left the city for a new home, a new life. Others have reinvented their country lifestyles—bed-and-breakfasts, antique shops, holiday retreats, kitchen gardens, even life under canvas! All share the desire for a quieter, greener life, open to new people, ideas, and experiences, rich in the (truly) finer things, a seedbed for long-lasting memories,

Bric-a-brac style

From cellar to attic, the country house is a treasure trove. Family memories, faded objects, forgotten furniture. Waiting to be salvaged, restored, and rediscovered by their delighted new owners, to create new interiors of their own.

in northern France
Setting the scene

Chez Andrée Leblanc
LA FERME D'AIGREMONT
(Bruxelles Antiques and Au Coin de la Reine)
Bric-a-brac, decoration, café
22, rue de la Reine, 59710 Ennevelin
www.bruxellesantiques.com
+ 33 (0)3 20 59 12 23

I have fond memories of the landscapes of northern France. The forests, pastureland, and rivers of Picardy and the Ardennes, cobbled streets and country roads threading between towns and fields. Here, in the village of Ennevelin, near the Belgian border, I chanced on a small corner of my childhood world—the Domaine d'Aigremont. The *domaine* itself—a fine eighteenth-century manor—has long since disappeared, although its imposing dovecote and drawbridge remain, leading to the home farm, surrounded by the original moat. Behind red brick walls and black-painted doors, Andrée has created a lifestyle that's worth the journey, whether browsing for bric-a-brac (tables patinated with age, faded bergères, lengths of galvanized lambrequin), taking inspiration from Andrée's decorative ideas, or enjoying a bite to eat at the adjoining café. The hands of a huge clock face stand fixed: savor the moment, a tantalizing taste of country living.

The shop sets the tone: restored workshop lamps,
a metal cupboard with its original, flaking paintwork,
an American office chair in battered leather.
Putting old objects to new uses, browsing, restoring.
Create the perfect room of your own—a place
to write, perhaps? Start a new page, tomorrow perhaps.

in Brittany
A family house

Chez Céline and Marc Lamour
LA MAISON DES LAMOUR
Bed-and-breakfast, holiday cottages
La Ville Guerfault, 22170 Plélo
www.lamaisondeslamour.com
+ 33 (0)2 96 79 51 25

Céline grew up here, in the Côtes d'Armor, where her parents Jeanne and Jean-Paul created a cheerful, bucolic retreat: the Char à Banc. An old mill, nestling at the bottom of a valley, renovated and restored over the years, a haven for families from far and wide. A place for lunch—a savory *potée* stew, or Breton pancakes; a place for pedal boats and pony rides. A place to stay and sleep, too, in the farmhouse next door, where Céline and Marc have labored to create a home-from-home for guests, friends, and their children. Around the square courtyard, each of the farm outbuildings has become a "guest house" open to the woods and fields. The main house reflects the couple's boundless talent and creativity, their flair for breathing new life into old objects, their insatiable passion for bric-a-brac and antique-hunting. From the entrance hall—dotted with sepia portraits—an ancient, patinated staircase leads to the former granary.

A streetlamp—salvaged from a street in Paris—hangs in the hallway
of the main house. Sliding metal panels open onto the dining room
and living room. Picture windows installed in the farm's rear walls look
onto the kitchen garden, which provides fresh vegetables for residents
and diners at the Char à Banc!

Gray, beige, white, and natural light. The walls of the smaller, cramped rooms have been knocked through. Wells of light pierce the wooden floor of the granary, illuminating the space. Slatted wooden side panels from an old cart form a balustrade. Every space bursts with Céline and Marc's unusual, offbeat ideas, inspired by their instinct to reuse and reycle, and their many finds at country bric-a-brac sales.

Old books and tattered pages

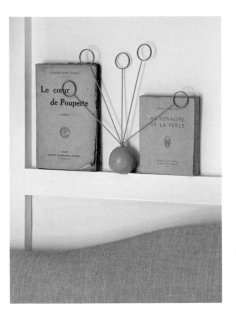  

The bedrooms are no exception—here, even stacks of old books and papers find new uses. Faded paperbacks
form a bedside table. Old novels, faded and foxed, become charming small pictures while they wait for
a new reader. Pages from a battered old school book are separated and hung one by one to form
a long, decorative frieze—a new chapter in the lively history of the Maison Lamour!

in Normandy

Off the superhighway

Christelle and David Lechevallier
BORD DE SCÈNE
Brocante and blog
23, rue de la Messe, Le Bray
27950 Villez-Sous-Bailleul
bord2scene.canalblog.com
+ 33 (0)2 32 52 46 18

Normandy. Garish light at the highway tollbooth. Overhead signs. The familiar images streaking by on the A13 highway west out of Paris, a road traveled so often, so fast. Slow down, take your time, play hooky. Take the Gaillon exit. Les Andelys, Château Gaillard, Giverny. Fleeting impressions of scenes already experienced. Surprise—an antiques and bric-a-brac store! It's a joy to stumble upon, but almost invisible from the road. Visitors are more likely to come across this small country business on the highways and byways of the blogosphere: its young, smiling owner, Christelle, is an Internet antiquer and bric-a-brac hunter, tracking down, patching up, patinating, and displaying her finds on the Web. Everything is beautifully displayed in Christelle's own home, a traditional *longère* nestling in the heart of a peaceful hamlet, discovered with delight by online buyers who travel here to collect their purchases. And since everything (or almost everything) is for sale, the decor is constantly changing—come again soon!

David and Christelle have reinvented their home as a store and showcase for their stock, incorporating their own living space—the kitchen and the series of bedrooms leading off one another under the eaves. Visitors are inquisitive—is this lamp for sale? You may have to wait for Christelle to unveil her next haul of treasures online, via her blog. There's no hurry!

in southwestern France
Green horizons

Chez Nathalie Guigné
LE RELAIS DE ROQUEFEREAU
Bed-and-breakfast, holiday cottages
Roquefereau, 47140 Penne d'Agenais
www.lerelaisderoquefereau.com
ı 33 (0)5 53 41 40 02

Nathalie has left town. Born into the fifth generation of a family of Parisian gallerists, she set out at the end of the 1990s to rediscover the landscapes of her childhood vacations. The Lot valley, Penne d'Agenais, a rich blend of nature and history. Here, she began a new life. In this rural setting, buying art isn't a high priority, so the gallerist turned antiques dealer. The green horizons of her daily drive became a part of life. And here, at the head of a small valley, she found this austere, majestic, beautiful building. The old medieval inn was solidly built, but the interior had suffered. After two years of work, Roquefereau was reborn. The new owner has opened gites and a bed-and-breakfast. Slate, linen, asphalt, pebbles—Nathalie has a feel for natural materials. Her home is clad in soft, subtle grays, enlivened here and there with touches of color—a painted canvas, an object—essential souvenirs of her former life, and her travels.

Roquefereau is serene and elegant, in its soft, pale palette of gray, taupe, and charcoal,

offset by white paint and limewash. A setting for a slower pace, where small details are observed

and appreciated: glass pendants, old jewelry, small pictures that tell a story. Outside, dinner is served

beneath the loggia, before the ever-changing spectacle of dusk embracing the valley.

In the "linen bedroom" crumpled sheets blend
with trompe l'oeil pillows painted on the wall itself.
An echo of the artist's pastel picture hanging
in the Suite d'Ardoise, brought here by Nathalie
from her Paris gallery.

north of the Loire
A rural retreat

Chez Clarisse and Arnaud de Saint-Martin
L'INDISCRET
Antiques and bric-a-brac
8, rue Basse, 28330 Authon-du-Perche
+ 33 (0)2 37 49 13 69

His Volvo is a familiar sight on the deep-set country roads of the Perche, southwest of Chartres. Behind the wheel is antiques dealer Arnaud de Saint-Martin, inveterate hunter of staircases, doors, and fireplaces. He adores the eighteenth century and fine natural materials. A chance real-estate advertisement brought him to a ruined *longère* in his native region: a dreamed-of idyll, a family home, a launchpad for new projects. The sale was speedily concluded, and the little farm began its metamorphosis. Flint walls were laid bare, some were knocked down. The surfaces were treated with limewash in the region's traditional yellow. New additions paid court to the existing, ancient house. The garden, enclosed by a hedge of pleached beech, was graced by a hideout for the children. Reawakened and restored, the house is now a gite, available to let for country weekends.

In the living room, traditional board games stand ready for a rainy Sunday afternoon.
Above a roaring fire, candles light up the elegant frame of a nineteenth-century overmantel.
Arnaud, a dedicated *brocanteur*, ensures nothing goes to waste: the kitchen units were cut down
from old doors and handles are fashioned from old cutlery. Upstairs, the old saloon-style doors
from a defunct cinema, La Dernière Séance, find new life. A children's paradise!

Board games for a rainy day

In the master bedroom, a Napoleon III armchair
has been reupholstered in purple fabric. A shoemaker's
last has been transformed into a lamp base. Arnaud
is full of ideas for bringing old objects back to life.

in Picardy

A distinctive home

Chez David Mistre
LA MAISON MISTRE
Guesthouse
3, rue de la Messe, 80270 Vergies
maison-mistre.blogspot.com
+ 33 (0)6 66 92 75 77

Antiques dealer and interior decorator Franck Delmarcelle has a naturally eclectic, inquisitive mind. Traveling back and forth between his Paris boutique and country retreat, he spotted this curious house in the heart of a Picardy village, for his friend David Mistre. Inspired by the Chinese pavilions greatly in vogue in the eighteenth century, the property stood out proudly from the neighboring brick-clad houses and farms. The weatherboarding and black foundations were reminiscent of seaside properties in the nearby Bay of the Somme—the perfect foil for Franck's decorative touch, his deep respect and passion for traditional techniques and expertise, expressed in his boundless enthusiasm for vintage bric-a-brac, with which he has furnished and decorated the house, from floor to ceiling! Beneath the porch, facing the main gate, a wrought-iron chair from a nineteenth-century garden suite is an invitation to bask in the sun and discover this distinctive guesthouse.

Dinner is served—in the basement! The kitchen is located in the former cellar,

while the garden peeks in at windows opened in the wall, for natural light.

As throughout the house, styles mix and mingle in perfect taste: a Louis XVI banquette,

a rustic farm table, an old grain sack in coarse linen laid us a tablecloth.

On the library walls, mirrors and frames are placed atop the wainscoting of plain, raw planks.
A console supports antique curiosities and a contemporary ceramic vase. A multicolored kilim
covers the floor. The accumulation of styles never strikes a wrong note—including the bedroom,
where Empire style sits perfectly with the quiet charm of the Picardy countryside.

in Anjou
A fairytale setting

Chez Nadège and Franck Dolais
QUATTROCENTO
Antiques
57, rue Georges-Clemenceau, 49150 Baugé
www.antiquites-quattrocento.com
+ 33 (0)9 60 50 56 58

Nadège and Franck are antiques dealers by profession. Chance naturally plays an important role in their day-to-day lives, like one special morning, which they still remember today. They had just discovered an old engraved portrait of the mayor of Baugé, a small town in Anjou, when they heard of a house for sale in the same town, 200 miles from their home! One visit was enough: they fell in love with the property at first sight. And the sixteenth-century building turned out to be the former home of—the mayor of Baugé! A sign? The couple quickly brought their fairytale world—part Italian Renaissance, part eighteenth century—to this new setting. With its walled garden, punctuated by a watchtower that once formed part of the town ramparts, the house and its outbuildings have undergone 400 years of change and transformation. Four hundred years? Like Quattrocento, the new name chosen by its present owners. A happy accident.

The couple's deceptively haphazard decorative choices reveal their shared passions:
every room overflows with mannequins used in traditional parades, fairground horses,
curios, and *objets de maîtrise* (created by craftsmen to demonstrate their skills).
A folding screen painted in shades of blue and ocher graces the sitting room. "We live and
breathe antiques, down to our forks and spoons!" smiles Franck. Nadège even uses old French
recipes and cookbooks in the kitchen. Will their young children follow suit?

For Félix, antiquing trips with his mother
are a crusade to "save teddy bears." And Pauline
invites her friends to play in her pastel-painted
bedroom, home to a vintage Mickey Mouse,
a rocking horse, and a four-poster bed worthy
of "The Princess and the Pea."

From the house to the shop, vintage bric-a-brac
comes and goes, seldom staying put for more than
a few days. What will become of this set of
multicolored Swedish chairs? Franck waits to see what
tomorrow will bring—ever ready to set a new scene.

Bohemian tastes

A house lives and grows over time, with new discoveries, new faces, the inspiration of the seasons. And imagination, the secret to a life less ordinary, closer to nature.

in the Auvergne

Art and old stones

Chez Marloes der Kinderen
LA GRANDE MAISON, ARTEDU
Bed-and-breakfast, restaurant, workshops
43300 Chanteuges
www.la-grande-maison.com
+ 33 (0)4 71 74 01 91

Bohemian tastes. The sound of an accordion is heard in the narrow lanes, lined with hollyhocks, of a village in the Auvergne. In this poetic moment, time stands still. Nihad is Bosnian. And an accordion player. He's rehearsing here, in the workshop at La Grande Maison, for a forthcoming concert in Amsterdam. The austere front facade of the building is impressive: five stories built in the fifteenth century, on the slopes of a rocky outcrop atop which stands the Romanesque abbey of Chanteuges. This seemingly raw setting has been brought back to life thanks to creative workshops run by Dutch painter Marloes der Kinderen. Steeped in the house's powerful atmosphere—it was once the home of a family of writers—Marloes has been careful to preserve its history. When she first moved in, the house was filled with objects, letters, and books, the source of her decorative inspiration.

A life-size canvas

Much of the furniture has never left the house. Marloes has also sourced pieces from around the region, and elsewhere in France, amassing myriad small collections in the process. Straw hats, terra-cotta pots, worn-out books, and dismembered picture frames are scattered throughout the house, like objects on a life-size canvas. On the floors, Marloes, an artist, has improvised graphic, engraved designs. The walls are hung with a multitude of small collages composed of fragments from the childhood writings of the house's former owner. Words and pictures that echo one another, linger and entice, like the accordion music fading gently in the narrow streets of Chanteuges, a place that's very hard to leave.

in the Alpilles
Deepest Provence

Chez Albine and Maurice Roumanille
LE MAS DOU PASTRE
Charming hotel, gypsy caravans
13810 Eygalières-en-Provence
www.masdupastre.com
+ 33 (0)4 90 95 92 61

It was twenty years ago at least—Albine and Maurice Roumanville remember it well. They have worked as antiques dealers, and tried their hands at other things, too. In the early 1990s, their parents left the family *mas*, its oldest stones dating back to the eighteenth century, at the foot of the Alpilles hills. To keep the house in the family, they decided to create a hotel, starting with just three rooms. Then six. Then their first gypsy caravan. In just five years, the hotel became a reference for the best in Provençal living. Truly a *hôtel de charme*, created by Albine and Maurice with a genuine sense of hospitality. "We did whatever felt right," says Albine. Bric-a-brac, vintage objects, and antiques are everywhere, of course. Furniture picked up in Provençal markets, collections of items found here and there: glass cloches and jars, zinc watering cans and jugs, and small flower paintings.

A collection of multicolored wine demijohns from
the 1950s adorns the sitting room.
Each bedroom has its own personality,
underscored with a particular color, a chestnut-wood
garden chair, a woven basket.

The garden is now home to three traditional gypsy
caravans: La Gitane, La Manouche, and La Voyageuse,
bought from traveling families, and the director
of a circus. The last word in bohemian style.

on the Atlantic coast
A residence reborn

Chez Pierre Casteleyn and Max Griffin
LE LOGIS DE PUYGATY & SORTI DE GRANGE
Bed-and-breakfast, decoration
16250 Chadurie
www.logisdepuygaty.com
+ 33 (0)5 45 21 75 11

A stony road crosses a vineyard. The top of a tower appears, through a gap in the hills. You have arrived at Puygaty. Passing through the entrance lodge, the main residence is discovered at the heart of a complex of fortified buildings. A journey into history. The house is thought to have been used by François I, as a summer residence. Other journeys, other eras: the house's new masters settled in Puygaty six years ago, after a nomadic existence in Belgium and Florida, a taste of the idle life, and vague plans to move to southern Italy. Finally, they dropped anchor in the quiet waters of Charentes, on France's central west coast. Their first years here were far from peaceful: work progressed from the main house to the barn. Roofs, doors, and windows needed replacing, walls had to be stripped and limewashed. All the renovation work was carried out using local artisans and techniques, retaining all of the building's great historic charm and character. Pale stonework, whitewashed wood, heavy wrought iron: the building's austere exterior gives little clue to what lies within.

Existing features have been left in their original state. The monumental fifteenth-century
fireplace still warms the living room of the main house. Guest rooms have been created in
the former stables. Drinking troughs, cribs, and mangers have been incorporated into the plain,
understated decor, with a focus on simple raw materials—and essential comforts, of course.

The hosts' refined taste creates a seamless blend of Louis XIII and Venetian styles,
with the simple forms of rustic furniture, folk art, and industrial chic. The space and objects
recovered in situ have naturally embraced finds sourced from all over the world.
As the renovation progressed, woodworkers proved hard to find. Pierre improvised by working
with the local blacksmith to create ingenious curtain rails, shelves, steps, and balustrades.

Stone, wood, metal, and fine linen

A host of functional or decorative objects in rusted metal fill the house. Pierre and Max have carried on working at the forge, creating their own collection of objects. Their chairs and stools are now available in their boutique and gallery in Puygaty, which also sells signed works by local ceramicists and cutlers. Not forgetting pairs of genuine Charentaise carpet slippers—perfect for visitors seeking rest and relaxation in this quiet place.

in Languedoc

The school of life

Chez Isabelle and Fred Remise
LA FONTAINE DE GRÉGOIRE
Guesthouse
Le Bourg, 15110 Saint-Urcize
www.aubrac-chezremise.com
+ 33 (0)4 71 23 20 02

The setting is rustic, the owner gruff—a "real character," you might think, on a first meeting. A product of the Aubrac mountain air, the reclusive life here in Saint-Urcize? He has a *buron* (a traditional shepherd's hut for making cheese) and a Citroën Mehari jeep. He's also the owner of a local institution, Chez Remise—a hotel, restaurant, bar, tobacco store, and newspaper stand run with his wife Isabelle, and family. The voluble band of local anglers have made it their headquarters. Fred Remise—for that is his name—knows every nook of the local river and mountain. Everyone knows him, too. And suddenly Saint-Urcize seems like the center of the world. Thanks to Fred, people came here first to fish. There were stirrings of life at the hotel. Then Fred and Isabelle renovated the old village school, in order to have bigger bedrooms. They gave it the name of the fountain on the village square. Now Saint-Urcize is a place of pilgrimage— not least for dinner chez Bras, in nearby Laguiole. Why not carry on to Santiago de Compostela? The old pilgrims' route passes further down the mountain.

A cosy, scholarly retreat

Where's Fred? Saint-Urcize is a small place, and Fred is never far from his hotel in the village's old school. Every morning, he's first up to light the fire in the great hearth, beside which stands "his" favorite armchair. The table stands in the midst of a space resembling a colorful, jumbled traveler's notebook in three dimensions: a cheerful accumulation of objects and vintage finds brought back from heaven knows where, each telling its own story.

Large volumes, carved panels, opulent bathrooms, and hidden touches of fantasy.

Fred and Isabelle have already devoted nine years to transforming the old school building,

which is destined for new plans in future. For the moment, everything is happening in the garden:

Fred has commissioned a student landscape gardener—his "protégé"—to redesign it, carte blanche.

The approach is typical of his profoundly humanist, philanthropic outlook. With a keen eye, too,

for the mountain and its wildflowers, the crucible of his personal school of (bohemian) life.

in La Perche
New rustic chic

Chez Armelle and Pierre Santarelli
L'HÔTEL DES TAILLES
Guest rooms
9 rue des Tailles, 61400 Mortagne-au-Perche
+ 33 (0)2 33 73 69 09

Saturday morning. The market-day crowds thread the busy streets of Mortagne-au-Perche, resplendent in Barbours and wellies, for a country weekend. Urban visitors do their best to blend in with La Perche's star village, west of Chartres. French lingerie designer Chantal Thomass has settled here for good. People are admiring the new decor of La Maison Fassier, now privately owned; lingering over lunch at La Vie en Rouge. Away from the beating heart of the village, those in the know meet at their very own *bar des amis*. The red lantern is lit—the Red Bar is open for business! Behind the counter at this informal bistro, Pierre has prepared a platter of cold meats to share, Armelle displays her latest vintage finds. Through the steamed-up windows, we glimpse the facade of their home, the Hôtel des Tailles. The talk is lively, and stories flow with the wine. If only this place could talk, too.

A judicious blend of styles

A fine eighteenth-century residence, the Hôtel Hocquart de Montfermeil was the house of the local tax collector, until the fall of the Ancien Régime. A few revolutions later, after many subsequent owners, it is the home of Armelle and Pierre Santarelli, the charming, unaffected hosts of this exceptional place. First, the guest rooms were installed on the upper floors. Next came the Red Bar and a small art gallery, improvised in the mansion's outbuildings. Everything reflects the owners' perfect taste and restraint. Industrial, ethnic, baroque, Provençal? The decor samples every possible style, with elegance and spontaneity.

Panelling in the dining room was stripped
and left untreated as a backdrop for panels
featuring hunting scenes, and a collection
of small pictures picked up here and there.
Opening off the dining room, a second salon
mixes industrial objects and ethnic art.

Crimson velvet, linen sheets, impeccable
white paint, and distressed wood: materials
and colors blend in the private world of travelers
Armelle and Pierre. They have lived in Provence,
and settled in La Perche, for the moment.
Tomorrow they may set out for new horizons.

A change of scene

New landscapes, a new home, fresh wall colors, a different plan for the furniture. Small details, to create unexpected new atmospheres.

An enlightened amateur

Chez Emmanuelle and Grégoire Courtin
VUE DE L'INTÉRIEUR
Bric-a-brac, antiques, home staging
7, rue du 8 mai 1945, 37370 Neuvy-le-Roi
www.vuedelinterieur.com
+ 33 (0)6 20 62 67 17

They seek him here, they seek him there. Always on the move, Grégoire Courtin plies the town's streets aboard a Segway, and even escapes down the country roads of Navarre, the surrounding region. Courtin is a *brocanteur*, an inquisitive collector, a "home stager," ever on the lookout for rare and unusual objects. His home is his intimate, personal museum. Armillary spheres, terrestrial globes, the accumulated collections of an enlightened amateur. Each carefully placed piece evokes a static journey. But times change: new finds, new projects inspire fresh changes of decor. A life-size saddler's horse, photographed in the living room, has already moved on to pastures new. The decorator always has a storehouse of new ideas up his sleeve. He loves novelty—he moves house often, as the mood takes him—but has never left the shores of the Loire, that bucolic crucible of French history. Renovating, creating color schemes, furnishing, improving: this is what he does best, as an inspired "revealer" of interiors.

A long monastery table, its top painted
black—mounted on casters because it was too
low—stands comfortably alongside an Ikea shelf
unit, its niches decorated with a Roman bust
and a collection of curios.

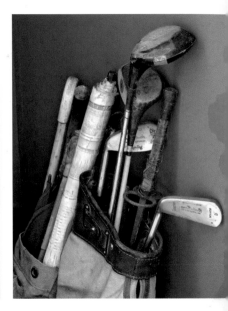

Green pepper, peat, black velvet, incense gray. Dark, muted colors offset
the accumulations of objects. A straw boater, fishing baskets, golf clubs,
piles of cream earthenware crockery, and—everywhere—books melt into the decor
of an outbuilding, which Grégoire lets to guests from time to time. The accommodation
offers modern comforts, too—a fitted fireplace and kitchen, and, of course,
the serene landscapes of the Tourangelle plain surrounding the village.

Naturally romantic

Chez Geneviève and Francis Coquet
LA MAISON DU BAILLI
Bed-and-breakfast
2, route de Courseulles, 14480 Villiers-le-Sec
www.ohotes.com/maisondubailli
+ 33 (0)2 31 37 61 70

Bayeux is famous for its long tapestry celebrating the Norman conquest of England by the French duke Guillaume (William the Conqueror). In the sixteenth century, the local bailiff lived here, midway between the regional capital at Bessin, and the beaches of the Côte de Nacre (the "mother-of-pearl coast"). The house has a rich history. Geneviève and Francis visited and bought it in the space of just twenty-four hours. Moving to the country from the western Paris suburb of Rambouillet, they originally planned to settle in the Pays d'Auge. But they weren't looking for a thatched cottage or second home. Both fell in love with La Maison du Bailli—a typical, elegant Bessin mansion, with its carriage house, cider barn, and stables, renovated by a previous English owner. All that needed changing was the decor. To brighten the austere facade, Geneviève called in a young artist from the Beaux-Arts to create a series of trompe l'oeil yew trees on the walls of Creully stone—bringing the garden right up the house. And that's the key to this delightful home, whose serene gardens are discovered beyond its high entrance arch. A sense of tranquility that seduced Geneviève and Francis, happy to live here in all seasons.

The interior is filled with Geneviève's bric-a-brac finds
and restored pieces, from Louis XIII to industrial chic,
repainted and arranged by the *maîtresse
de maison*—something she loves doing. Right now,
she's considering a more contemporary look.

Ce soir ou jamais, Petite chérie—each bedroom bears the name
of a fragrance. Geneviève leaves subtle clues, phrases dotted here and there,
handwritten on pebbles lying in trails, like breadcrumbs on a forest path.

in the Périgord
Flemish elegance

Chez Jan van Grinsven
CHÂTEAU LES MERLES
Hotel, bistro lounge, spa, and golf course
Tuilières, 24520 Mouleydier
www.lesmerles.com
+ 33 (0)5 53 63 13 42

White Heather, a thirty-five-meter sailing yacht. And her skipper, Jan van Grinsven. A latterday explorer. One man and his boat—with the family all aboard—traversed the oceans before dropping anchor on the banks of the Dordogne River and falling in love. The object of his desire was a seventeenth-century charterhouse nestled languidly in a hollow of the Périgourdine hills, planted with vineyards. The dreamer's voyage continues, amid the calm reaches of the Domaine des Merles. The *White Heather* is close at hand—in the form of a model, displayed in the gourmet lounge bistro, named in French for its owner's former ship—*La Bruyère blanche*. The estate has its own vineyards and winery, a golf course, spa, and, of course, a hotel. An ambitious program, but unostentatious, on a resolutely human, personal scale. Because life at the domaine is a family affair: Jan's three daughters all live and work here, too.

 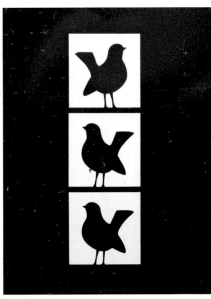 

The decor is the work of the captain's brother, the artist and sculptor
Joris van Grinsven. The charterhouse's volumes, atmosphere,
and original structure have been subtly underscored with an elegant
black-and-white scheme, heightened with eclectic "designer" touches,
baroque elements, dashes of color, and a hint of Flemish culture,
thanks to reproductions of works by the great Flemish masters.

White walls, black floors. Touches of fuchsia
pink and anise green enliven the restful,
monastic atmosphere.

in Burgundy
Colorful interiors

Chez Barbara van Stek and Hans van Braak
LA ROSERAIE
Restaurant, guest rooms, holiday cottage
Le Bourg, 71540 Lucenay-l'Évêque
www.laroseraie.nl
+ 33 (0)3 85 82 68 95

Barbara and Hans are inveterate travelers. From Canada to Australia and finally here, to a peaceful village in the Morvan national park, a place of lakes and forests, lush meadows and rippling streams. The couple fell in love with the region, and embarked on a new adventure with the purchase of a run-down old inn. Everything "needed doing," but after several months of intensive work, La Roseraie was up and running once again. A small, quiet river, the Ternin, flows peacefully at the bottom of their flower-filled garden—roses, of course. Hans has created a holiday house, for guests; Barbara has added a kitchen garden for seasonal, organic fruit and vegetables, used in her inventive recipes served in the cheerful restaurant—bright salads and an endless array of tapas. Word of mouth has brought a stream of visitors to enjoy this slice of reinvented life, which opens in the summer months only. Barbara and Hans have other projects lined up: another journey, perhaps another move. A book for sure, which Barbara is currently finishing: *Food for the Soul*, a collection of inspired, heart-warming recipes.

In the library, books and travel guides are cleverly arranged to recreate the colors of the rainbow. Yellow, green, blue, and red—each one a slice of life to savor at leisure. Pages to turn in eager anticipation of the next, unexpected chapter; a tribute to Barbara and Hans's colorful, imaginative approach.

A subtle blend
of light and color

Slate, pearl, clay, elephant-hide, taupe, mat white, and lacquered black—La Roseraie is
a light-filled setting decorated in soft, neutral shades with bold touches of color, and the yin and yang contrast
of black-and-white checkered wallpapers, or plain paintwork. Constantly changing collections of recycled
furniture finds, home-made pieces, and clever DIY-deco ideas—including a brilliant system of chandeliers
which can be adjusted for height and light—contribute their own style and ambience.
The evanescent moods of a simple life, lived day by day, for the moment.

in Alsace

A vintage paradise

Chez Nathalie and Frédéric Langel
UN SOIR D'ÉTÉ
Guesthouse
19, rue Haute, 67120 Ernolsheim-sur-Bruche
www.unsoir-d-ete.com
+ 33 (0)6 07 96 90 67

A May evening. The annual jumble and bric-a-brac sale in the village of Ernolsheim draws to a close. As usual, Nathalie and Frédéric have set out their stall, selling some of their surplus accumulations of objects. They've made some new finds, too—both adore hunting for antiques and vintage pieces. It's a passion, and a way of life, filling their "home museum" with folk art, and twentieth-century decorative and consumer objects: a temple to vintage design. A shrine to sustainability, too, where discarded and forgotten objects are revived and put to new uses, saving them from the bin. And an eminently practical approach, thanks to which the couple have furnished virtually the whole of their Alsatian farmhouse, their home for the past three years. Goodbye to city life! Nathalie and Frédéric are freelancers, young parents, and committed environmentalists. Here, they have found the pace of life they dreamed of. Fred is finishing work on his renovated photography studio, Nathalie runs her advertising agency from home. And their guesthouse brings the rest of the world to their doorstep.

Overlooking the farmyard, the whole house
is open to guests. Half-timbered charm outside,
vintage style within: 1950s sideboards,
1970s ornaments, even vinyl LPs from the 1980s,
the decor prompts memories of times not
so very long past.

Bertoia, Rietveld: each guest room is a tribute to Nathalie and Fred's favorite pieces, and their designers. They might equally well have been named Jacobsen, Prouvé, Mondrian, et al. In addition to vintage pieces of museum quality, the couple collects colorful souvenirs from the heyday of twentieth-century consumerism, the Plastic Years, the years of their teens. Articulated robots and action figures inspired by TV shows of the period, electric wall clocks of all shapes and sizes, rotary dial telephones. Timeless memories.

in the Gironde valley
An artist's inspiration

Chez Cyril de Commarque
LE PRESSOIR
Country house for short rentals
Domaine du Château de La Bourlie, 24480 Urval
www.chateaudelabourlie.com
+ 33 (0)6 07 10 00 56

Sometimes, a glance at the small ads of a daily newspaper can be the key to a new country life. The advertisement in question—three lines that caught the eye of an urban reader hungry for greenery—announced a "country house for rent, near the market town of Sarlat, sleeps 6–10. Le Pressoir." One telephone call and a trip to the Périgord later, our reader found himself the proud owner of the eponymous "wine press"—a stunning property flanked by a mill race, below the landscaped park of the Château de la Bourlie, officially classified as one of France's *Jardins Remarquables*. A barn, a mill, and three ranges of buildings dating back to the fourteenth century. Cyril de Commarque began restoring the place his way—"barefoot," in touch with nature. An artist, videomaker, and photographer, Cyril has lived in Paris, London, and New York. Now, he's putting down roots and finding inspiration on the upper reaches of the Gironde, the so-called Périgord Pourpre.

Le Pressoir offers spacious volumes, from the living room to the bedrooms. Natural raw materials, vintage Danish furniture, kilims sourced from a souk in Tunis, and pieces made from wood gleaned on the estate. Simple but elegant, the decor inspires a feeling of serenity.

Back to basics

Rediscover a taste for simple pleasures.
Be the master of your own time.
Invent a new existence, focused on life's
essentials—on the farm, in an ecolodge,
under canvas. Nature on your doorstep.

in northern Brittany

Among the flowers of the field

Chez Liz and Corentin Lamour
PETITES MAISONS DANS LA PRAIRIE
Bed-and-breakfast, holiday cottages
Le Mourvet Noir, 22170 Plélo
www.roselouisemarie.com
+ 33 (0)2 96 79 52 39

It's a family affair: we've met Céline and Marc, owners of that essential country retreat, the Char à banc. Now meet Corentin and Liz, at Plélo, a blissful hamlet nestling between the Atlantic and the lush Brittany countryside. With a nod to childhood memories, the couple have named their gites the "little houses on the prairie": seven cozy holiday cottages surrounded by a farm, fields of cows, meadows of tall grass dotted with cosmos flowers. Choose from Rose, Florence, Marie, Louise, Joséphine, Anne, and Jeanne—each stone cottage is named for a grandmother, a great aunt, or a dear neighbor. And each of the seven "queens of hearts" has actually lived in one of these traditional Breton longhouses. Corentin's mother Jeanne was even born here. When Irish-born Liz arrived from Cork to perfect her French, she stole his heart away.

Seven little houses, full of delights

Corentin and Liz began by renovating one of the cottages as their home. Corentin took charge of the farm and its animals, and little by little each cottage was restored. The walls are insulated with natural limewash and hemp from the fields; farm objects have been recycled, pieces of furniture picked up here and there. Liz brings her personal charm and creativity to the decor. Painted wooden floors, checkered tiles, doors pierced with a scattering of cut-out hearts, garlands of lights, and always a bouquet of fresh wildflowers. An irresistible call to pack your bags and take to the fields.

Wild herbs, organic produce, warm summer nights

Chez Isabella Salusti
GRAINE ET FICELLE
Garden produce, cooking classes,
guest rooms and farmhouse meals, ecolodge
670, chemin des Collets, 06640 Saint-Jeannet
www.graine-ficelle.com
+ 33 (0)6 85 08 15 64

The donkeys are named Estaban, Chiquito, Poncho, and Lila. The cow goes by the name of Roquette. Isabella is Italian—from Rome—a young, energetic former stylist who has retreated to Saint-Jeannet from life in the big city. Back to nature—the simple life, in the herb-scented backcountry of the Côte d'Azur. On the site of an ancient, stone shepherd's hut, Isabella has created a house open to the region's dazzling light, and an organic farm. A madcap scheme that is gradually taking root: a kitchen garden, free-range animals, a new life. Guided farm visits for children and school groups, a guesthouse, cooking classes, wine tastings. A hectic schedule! And a host of projects and plans in the offing. Isabella's kitchen has been featured on TV—her past is catching up with her!

In the mountains north of Nice, Isabella's home boasts stunning views of the distant
Mediterranean. The kitchen—the heart of the farm—was the first space to be completed.
Since then the operation has grown, little by little: a natural swimming pool, a greenhouse,
a jam-making workshop. Peppers, zucchini, and green beans are favorite ingredients
for Isabella's exceptional vegetable preserves, in huge demand from Nice's top chefs—who have
become clients and friends, sharing their expertise through cooking classes offered at the farm.

Fine cuisine, to the letter

Isabella's first visitors came to sample her organic farmhouse cooking, learn a new recipe, the tricks of the trade. The lunches got longer—now guests come to spend a day in the country, a night or two in one of the guest rooms, or the ecolodges: comfortable tented pavilions installed nearby (meals are taken at the farm). There are even plans for a new ecohouse on the site.

in Poitou-Charentes: the French Mid-West
An organic oasis

Chez Olivia and Jean-Philippe Gautier
LES ORANGERIES
Ecological hotel and restaurant
12, avenue du Docteur Dupont
86320 Lussac-les-Châteaux
www.lesorangeries.fr
+ 33 (0)5 49 84 07 07

Angers, Poitiers, Limoges. Towns that too many travelers know only as signposts off France's southbound routes, choked with summer vacationers heading for the Mediterranean. But some will turn off here, where the road falls into step with the valley of the river Vienne, and head for the village of Lussac-les-Châteaux, the birthplace of Madame de Montespan. An oasis. A mirage, perhaps? No, ideed: the village is home to France's first officially recognized ecohotel, a gem discovered by pioneering guests back in the late 1990s, when Olivia and Jean-Philippe launched a charming hotel in a seventeenth-century house belonging to the family, dedicated to sustainable development and a certain art of fine living. Jean-Philippe has fond memories of family vacations here as a child. Now an architect, he took charge of renovating and refurbishing the hotel, taking account of the necessary rules and regulations (of course), but also his personal skills and beliefs. Materials were sourced locally, often recycled, the walls were insulated with hemp, and the interior surfaces were coated with limewash colored using natural pigments. Each new extension or enhancement follows the same philosophy—the guiding principle of daily life in this special place, too.

The decor is Olivia's domain. The hotel's lively chatelaine is a fervent devotee
of sustainable tourism and development: vintage furniture and objects are hunted
down and restored, fabrics and drapes feature warm, vivid colors. Motifs give
a discreet nod to the orange trees that fill the hotel's landscaped gardens.

A shared passion

Olivia's commitment to sustainable tourism is shared by the entire hotel team,
including the young chef, whose superb dishes use seasonal local
produce—mainly organic—from nearby kitchen gardens.

on the banks of the Loire
New life on the farm

Chez Anna, Agatha, Sophie,
and Jean-Luc Guignard
LES GÎTES DE L'ÉTANG DES NOUES
Bed-and-breakfast, holiday cottages
La Grollerie, L'Étang des Noues, 49300 Cholet
www.lesgitesdeletangdesnoues.com
+ 33 (0)2 41 58 87 53

La Grollerie is a five-hundred-year-old farmhouse in the heart of the Mauges, a historic region of rolling hills, valleys, and pastureland near the town of Cholet, south of the Loire—a place even the most determined GPS might be hard pushed to locate. Today, the building is enjoying a new lease on life in the hands of Sophie and Jean-Luc—country children born and bred, teen rebels, and dreamers (Sophie spent time in the northern English city of Leeds, Jean-Luc played in a rock band) and now—following the birth of their daughter, Anna—the proud rebuilders and restorers of this ancient farm, taking them back to their rural roots. Complementing the farm's two gites, the couple have begun keeping animals, just for fun: donkeys, ducks, Angora goats, and Ouessant sheep enjoy the tender loving care of their owners, and their guests' children, who are encouraged to feed, pet, and help look after them. Simple, everyday activities for grown-ups and children to share, on the shores of a small lake, the Étang des Noues.

Maison de coton, maison de lin: Sophie and Jean-Luc have created two guesthouses, available *à la carte* for anything from a single night to several weeks. Guests are made to feel completely at home, with attentive personal touches, cozy rustic comforts, embroidered linen, and farmhouse meals on request. A new approach to life on the farm: rustic but eminently comfortable, content with simple, shared pleasures. A utopian dream that has become reality.

Authentic rustic charm

No farm is complete without its farmyard animals:
a crowing cock, fresh eggs, a friendly Mother Duck
(by the name of Josephine) herding her army
of ducklings. Rustic delights, day after day.

in the southern Massif Central
A new beginning

Chez Amélie and Thomas
LA FERME DES CHAMPEAUX
Un Lit au Pré
87120 Saint-Amand-le-Petit
www.unlitaupre.fr
+ 33 (0)1 41 31 08 00

We had read the brochure over and again, noting all the practical details of our planned stay under canvas, deep in the countryside: a blissful country break as promised by the team at Un Lit au Pré, the French arm of the international Feather Down Farm network. We knew what to expect. But arriving at La Ferme des Champeaux was a surprise nonetheless. Owners Amélie and Thomas showed us around our tent: 430 square feet under canvas, with wooden floors, two bedrooms, a cozy boxed-in bed, a wooden worktop, and a wood-burning stove. The children raced down the sloping meadow to play with Viane, Paco, and Luc (who are lucky enough to live here all year round). We didn't see them again until it was time for dinner, eaten by the light of candles and an oil lamp. Nightfall, and the dying embers of the fire. Early next morning, a fine view of the surrounding mountains and the Plateau de Millevaches greeted our amazed, citydwellers' eyes. Drinking in the landscape, collecting eggs, fetching milk, walking in the forest, swimming in the lake, collecting wood, lighting the fire. Simple tasks performed every day for a week, yet no two days were the same. And that was all we did: nothing, except share a slice of Thomas and Amélie's lives. Unforgettable moments in an idyllic rural home.

The perfect, picture-postcard country holiday—and memories to last a lifetime. Feather Down Farm vacations were launched in 2003 by Dutch businessman Luite Moraal, a citydweller determined to realize his childhood dream of a cabin in the woods. A dozen prototypes were tried and tested before Feather Down planted its first tent, on a farm in the Netherlands. Each participating farm is chosen with care, reflecting their owners' shared ideals: to help people get back to the soil, and discover the delights of a simpler, greener lifestyle.

Everyday tasks, simple details

Each tent has running water. To heat it, guests light their own wood-burning stove.
Newcomers take time to get accustomed, but quickly establish a routine, learning to take life at
a slower, simpler pace. A true luxury! The luxury of simplicity: the rustic, recycled decor shows
attention to detail, and a genuine concern for comfort. Children fight over the "bed-box"
(no camp beds here). There's a big pitcher for fresh milk, enameled tableware, a kettle,
neat rows of egg cups, a traditional larder. The essentials of daily life.

But no electricity! Coffee is ground in an old-fashioned grinder, and supplies can be bought from the grocery store on site (the shower block is installed next door): freshly ground coffee, store-cupboard basics, fresh produce, bread, and pastries all made at the farm. A self-sufficient paradise, far from the madding crowd and its constant race against the clock. Rediscover the joys of living simply, day by day. A new beginning.

Address book

Alsace

Near Strasbourg
UN SOIR D'ÉTÉ page 152
Guesthouse
19, rue Haute, 67120 Ernolsheim-sur-Bruche
www.unsoir-d-ete.com
+ 33 (0)6 07 96 90 67

Aquitaine

Near Bergerac
CHÂTEAU LES MERLES page 136
Hotel, bistro lounge, spa, and golf course
Tuilières, 24520 Mouleydier
www.lesmerles.com
+ 33 (0)5 53 63 13 42

Near Sarlat
LE PRESSOIR page 160
Country house for short rentals
Domaine du Château de La Bourlie, 24480 Urval
www.chateaudelabourlie.com
+ 33 (0)6 07 10 00 56

Near Agen
LE RELAIS DE ROQUEFEREAU page 35
Bed-and-breakfast, holiday cottages
Roquefereau, 47140 Penne-d'Agenais
www.lerelaisderoquefereau.com
+ 33 (0)5 53 41 40 62

Auvergne

Near Laguiole
LA FONTAINE DE GRÉGOIRE page 98
Guesthouse
Le Bourg, 15110 Saint-Urcize
www.aubrac-chezremise.com
+ 33 (0)4 71 23 20 02

Near Puy-en-Velay
LA GRANDE MAISON, ARTEDU page 72
Bed-and-breakfast, restaurant, workshops
43300 Chanteuges
www.la-grande-maison.com
+ 33 (0)4 71 74 01 91

Burgundy

Near Autun
LA ROSERAIE page 144
Restaurant, guest rooms, holiday cottage
Le Bourg, 71540 Lucenay-l'Évêque
www.laroseraie.nl
+ 33 (0)3 85 82 68 95

Brittany

Near Saint-Brieuc
LA MAISON DES LAMOUR page 18
Bed-and-breakfast, holiday cottages
La Ville Guerfault, 22170 Plélo
www.lamaisondeslamour.com
+ 33 (0)2 96 79 51 25

Near Saint-Brieuc
PETITES MAISONS DANS LA PRAIRIE page 170
Bed-and-breakfast, holiday cottages
Le Mourvet Noir, 22170 Plélo
www.roselouisemarie.com
+ 33 (0)2 96 79 52 39

Central France

Near Nogent-le-Rotrou
L'INDISCRET page 44
Antiques and bric-a-brac
8, rue Basse
28330 Authon-du-Perche
+ 33 (0)2 37 49 13 69

Near Tours
VUE DE L'INTÉRIEUR page 122
Bric-a-brac, antiques, home staging
7, rue du 8 mai 1945, 37370 Neuvy-le-Roi
www.vuedelinterieur.com
+ 33 (0)6 20 62 67 17

Limousin

Near Limoges
LA FERME DES CHAMPEAUX page 196
Un Lit au Pré
87120 Saint-Amand-le-Petit
www.unlitaupre.com and www.featherdown.com
+ 33 (0)1 41 31 08 00

Nord-Pas-de-Calais

Near Lille
LA FERME D'AIGREMONT page 10
Bric-a-brac, decoration, café
22, rue de la Reine, 59710 Ennevelin
www.bruxellesantiques.com
+ 33 (0)3 20 59 12 23

Normandy

Near Vernon
BORD DE SCÈNE page 28
Brocante and blog
23, rue de la Masse, Le Bray
27950 Villez-sous-Bailleul
bord2scene.canalblog.com
+ 33 (0)2 32 52 46 18

Neur Alençon
L'HÔTEL DES TAILLES page 108
Guest rooms
9, rue des Tailles
61400 Mortagne-au-Perche
+ 33 (0)2 33 73 69 09

Near Caen
LA MAISON DU BAILLI page 131
Bed-and-breakfast
2, route de Courseulles, 14480 Villiers-le-Sec
www.ohotes.com/maisondubailli
+ 33 (0)2 31 37 61 70

The Loire

Near Angers
LES GÎTES DE L'ÉTANG DES NOUES page 191
Bed-and-breakfast, holiday cottages
La Grollerie, L'Etang des Noues, 49300 Cholet
www.lesgitesdeletangdesnoues.com
+ 33 (0)2 41 58 87 53

Near Saumur
QUATTROCENTO page 60
Antiques
57, rue Georges-Clemenceau, 49150 Baugé
www.antiquites-quattrocento.com
+ 33 (0)9 60 50 56 58

Poitou-Charentes

Near Angoulême
LE LOGIS DE PUYGATY & SORTI DE GRANGE page 89
Bed-and-breakfast, decoration
16250 Chadurie
www.logisdepuygaty.com
+ 33 (0)5 45 21 75 11

Near Poitiers
LES ORANGERIES page 184
Ecological hotel and restaurant
12, avenue du Docteur Dupont,
86320 Lussac-les-Châteaux
www.lesorangeries.fr
+ 33 (0)5 49 84 07 07

Picardy

Near Abbeville
LA MAISON MISTRE page 50
Guesthouse
3, rue de la Messe, 80270 Vergies
maison-mistre.blogspot.com
+ 33 (0)6 66 92 75 77

Provence and the Côte d'Azur

Near Nice
GRAINE ET FICELLE page 177
Garden produce, cooking classes, guest rooms and
farmhouse meals, ecolodge
670, chemin des Collets, 06640 Saint-Jeannet
www.graine-ficelle.com
+ 33 (0)6 85 08 15 64

Near Aix-en-Provence
LE MAS DOU PASTRE page 80
Charming hotel, gypsy caravans
13810 Eygalières-en-Provence
www.masdupastre.com
+ 33 (0)4 90 95 92 61 80

Thanks

To France's regional and departmental tourist offices, for their warm welcome

Alsace, www.tourisme-alsace.com
Anjou, www.anjou-tourisme.com
Aquitaine, www.tourisme-aquitaine.fr
Burgundy, www.bourgogne-tourisme.com
Nord, Pas-de-Calais, www.tourisme-nordpasdecalais.fr
Centre, www.visaloire.com
Calvados, www.calvados-tourisme.com
Cantal, www.cantaltourisme.fr
Dordogne, www.dordogne-perigord.com
Lot-et-Garonne, www.tourisme-lotetgaronne.com
Orne, www.ornetourisme.com
Pays-de-la-Loire, www.enpaysdelaloire.com
Provence, Alpes et Côte d'Azur, www.crt-riviera.fr and www.decouverte-paca.fr
Saône-et-Loire, www.bourgogne-du-sud.com
Vienne, www.tourisme-vienne.com

To Farrow and Ball for the wallpaper visuals from the Tented Stripe Collection, featured at the start of each chapter.

Farrow & Ball Showrooms:
New York, Greenwich, Boston, Los Angeles, Washington, and Chicago, + 1 (888) 511-1121.
www.farrow-ball.com

and especially to
Delphine Bartier, Sylvie Blin, Sophie Bougeard, Cécile Broc, Sophie Brugerolles, Anne Dessery, Guillaume Doury, Sylvie Favat, Anne Fernandez, Sabine Canonica, Alain Étienne, Marie-Yvonne Holley, Armelle Jouan, Christine Kervadec, Armelle Le Goff, Micheline Morissonneau, Ghislain Mouraux, Patricia de Pouzilhac, Virginie Priou, Jenny Seibert, Hélène Ramsamy, and Carole Rauber

To the team at Flammarion

To my family and friends, to the readers of my previous publications—in particular *Vintage French Interiors* and *French Style at Home*—and to the secret passengers of my Volvo road trips for their silent support.

Conception and Design: Sébastien Siraudeau

Blog: *(dans le coffre de la volvo)*, inmyvolvocar.blogspot.com

Editorial Direction: Ghislaine Bavoillot

Translated from the French by Louise Rogers Lalaurie

Copyediting: Helen Woodhall

Typesetting: Gravemaker + Scott

Proofreading: Chrisoula Petridis

Color Separation: IGS, L'isle d'Espagnac, France

Distributed in North America by Rizzoli International Publications, Inc.

Simultaneously published in French as *Vivre au Vert: Un nouvel art de vivre*

© Flammarion, SA, Paris, 2010

English-language edition

© Flammarion, SA, 2010

editions.flammarion.com

10 11 12 13   4 3 2 1

ISBN: 9782080301345

Dépôt légal: 04/2010

Printed in Slovenia by Korotan